DATE DUE

Saint Augustine
And The
Augustinian Tradition

PRESENTED UNDER THE AUSPICES OF

Villanova University

UNDER THE EDITORSHIP OF

Robert P. Russell, O.S.A

THE SAINT AUGUSTINE LECTURE 1962

At the Origins
of the
Thomistic Notion
of Man

by *Anton C. Pegis*, F.R.S.C., LL.D.

Professor of the History of Philosophy
Pontifical Institute of Mediaeval Studies
Toronto

THE MACMILLAN COMPANY, NEW YORK
COLLIER-MACMILLAN LIMITED, LONDON

Nihil obstat
  Edward J. Montano, S.T.D.
  Censor Librorum
Imprimatur
  ✠ Francis Cardinal Spellman
  Archbishop of New York
March 21, 1963

The Macmillan Company, New York
Collier-Macmillan Canada Ltd., Toronto, Ontario
Library of Congress catalog card number: 63-15693
Printed in the United States of America

CONTENTS

INTRODUCTION

The Saint Augustine Lecture is presented annually by Villanova University and is dedicated to the theme of "Saint Augustine and the Augustinian Tradition." In keeping with its basic aim, namely, to promote a better understanding of the teachings and influence of Augustine, outstanding scholars from here and abroad are invited each year to discuss some significant and timely aspect of this vast and rich intellectual heritage.

In the domain of Christian philosophy, Dr. Anton Pegis is well known as a teacher, editor, and lecturer. More recently, he has turned his attention to the problem of developing and formulating a Thomistic anthropology, or philosophy of man. His researches into St. Augustine and medieval Augustinianism stemmed from a natural effort to discover the decisive influence that enabled Aquinas to transform the Aristotelian notion of man and thereby to create a doctrine which "in its spiritual framework and substance" seems nearer to St. Augustine than it was to Aristotle. In the pages that follow, Dr. Pegis offers us in concise and convincing language those reflections and deep insights that led him to conclude that Augustine of Hippo is indeed the "key" to the doctrine of man in the philosophy of the Angelic Doctor.

ROBERT P. RUSSELL, O.S.A.

Villanova University
Villanova, Pennsylvania

At the Origins of the

THOMISTIC NOTION of MAN

Part I

THERE IS no fundamental disagreement among the students of St. Thomas on his view that the human soul, which is an intellectual substance in its own right, is also, in its essence, the unique substantial form of the human body. But this teaching, which to St. Thomas is the only one that can properly express the unity of man as a composite substance, is presented by him not only in the Aristotelian language of the *Metaphysics* and the *De Anima* but also as an Aristotelian doctrine. Now, this historical contention is far from evident. There are good reasons for thinking that St. Thomas' supposed Aristotelianism on the unity of man is not Aristotelian either in the data of the problem or in the proposed solution. It was St. Thomas and not Aristotle who visualized both the problem to be solved and the Aristotelian setting for its analysis and solution. In other words, Aristotle supplied certain metaphysical notions guaranteeing against Plato the unity of composite substances;

3

Aristotle did not supply any view of man requiring that an intellectual soul and an organic body be conceived in the light of such metaphysical notions. Such will be the argument of the present lecture.[1]

Those who, following the lead of St. Thomas himself, are willing to piece Aristotelian texts together in order to show that the Philosopher held the same doctrines that St. Thomas expounds with his words do not realize how much St. Thomas created the very Aristotelianism that he gives the impression of merely interpreting; nor do they realize that the battle over Aristotle in the thirteenth century was not a simple matter of expounding in a straightforward way a straightforward Aristotelian philosophical text. If St. Thomas was able to prove against Averroës that on specific points the Commentator was doing violence to Aristotle, this victory was very far from being a positive interpretation of Aristotle's psychology as a whole; and when St. Thomas faced such a task in his own turn, he not only created that baffling Philosopher whose name appears so frequently in the Thomistic writings; he also gave to him a metaphysical setting and foundation that the ancient Stagirite never knew. In short, St. Thomas' Aristotle is a Thomistic creation, and a perfectly possible one. Indeed, it is so possible that many students have found it difficult to discover any Aristotle other than St. Thomas' creation. Only, let us not deny to a Christian theologian either his creative originality as an interpreter of Aristotle or his concern to use Aristotelian ideas in the exposition of Christian religious truths. Let us even recognize that the Thomistic conception of man, which is

4

expressed so confidently by its author in Aristotelian terms, is nevertheless a doctrine that none of the great commentators before St. Thomas—not Alexander, not Avicenna, not Averroës—had visualized as philosophically possible in Aristotelian terms. None of them believed that an intellectual substance could be in its very essence the substantial form of matter. What, then, led St. Thomas to conceive as a doctrinal possibility a notion that no outstanding Aristotelian before him had found in the text of Aristotle? How did he come to ask whether the human soul, considered precisely in its nature as a self-subsistent intellectual substance, was related to the human body in the way in which, within the world of purely material bodies, forms are related to matter?

A first answer to this question consists in saying that the Aristotelian notions of form and matter had only to live within a metaphysics of being as act, and to be applied to man as seen within the perspective of the Christian doctrine of creation, in order to lead to the Thomistic view of the unity of man and his nature.[2] This is, in fact, what happened. According to St. Thomas, the existence of the human soul as form of the body, far from being engulfed by the body, rather raises matter to a spiritual existence and a spiritual life; as a result, within the soul's spiritual existence, there is constituted the most paradoxical of all creatures, man himself, a composite of spirit and matter living wholly and uniquely with a spiritual existence. But what this answer does not explain is how the doctrine could have happened at all. If the Aristotelians did not think it possible, and if St. Thomas' fellow theologians agreed that it was not possible, what enabled St. Thomas to follow such an unpromising philosophical direction and to call it Aristotelian?

If St. Thomas had merely made his own the current Aristotelian notions of matter and form as a convenient language in which to express the relations between soul and body, but without adopting the very point that finally drove other Aristotelians (and the thirteenth century theologians after them) away from a strict understanding of the language used, then it would be much easier to appreciate the phenomenon before us. But St. Thomas is distinguished from other students of Aristotle because he accepted, whereas they rejected, the full meaning and consequences of saying that the intellectual soul is in its very essence the form of matter, constituting with it one substance called man. And this is an entirely noteworthy distinction. Only, what enabled St. Thomas to visualize man in this way—I mean to say, to visualize in philosophical terms a notion that he then thought to express with full adequacy in the Aristotelian doctrine of matter and form? What enabled him to think not only that soul and body could be joined together as parts within a single existence, that of the soul, but also that they could constitute a single and unique essence whose mutually proportioned parts they were and without which they both remained unintelligible? What led St. Thomas to argue that the human soul had in the very structure of its intellectual nature the need to be completed by an organic body, to argue as a consequence that the body itself had in its constitution as a body the nature to be completed by an

6

intellectual soul, and to visualize the unity of man not as a consequence of the parts constituting him but as the intelligible whole that ultimately gave meaning to the parts themselves? For St. Thomas did not arrive at the unity of man by simply manufacturing a composite made up of soul and body; he arrived at the meaning of soul and body from a certain conception of man, and the question is to know the origin of that conception. It may be that St. Thomas simply created such a philosophical doctrine, in which case the possibility of the doctrine must be held to rest on his vision. Only, was there not at hand a notion of man that could lead him to express the unity of man within an Aristotelian formula and to explore, with unprecedented metaphysical inventiveness, the union of an immaterial soul and a material body as though they were intelligible parts of an Aristotelian essence, even though Aristotle himself had never posited such an essence?

We have inherited two great psychologies from the ancient world, the moral psychology of Plato and the biological psychology of Aristotle. But we have likewise inherited centuries of late ancient and Christian speculation on these two views of man. The Platonic view of man, in particular, was the occasion of a remarkable fusion of philosophical ideas and ascetical and spiritual themes, producing not only a wealth of imagery that went far beyond the thought or the text of Plato but also a religious psychology in which the Platonic philosophical elements served the spiritual and contemplative aims of their Christian authors. The result of this fusion can be seen in St.

Augustine and in the Cistercian and Victorine writers of the twelfth century. But the religious character of the fusion is as noteworthy in its own right as the use made by these writers of the Platonic tag that man is a soul using a body.[3] When the thirteenth century opened, the psychology of Aristotle, so biological in its approach to man and so rooted in metaphysical considerations in its explanation of the human composite, introduced not only a new dimension into Christian thought on the nature and constitution of man but also a new moment in the history of Platonism and especially the Christian Platonism of the Augustinian tradition.

It was one thing to use the Platonic notion of man for purposes of religious meditation; indeed, by its remarkable emphasis on the interior ordering of man and his life the Platonic psychology readily lent itself to the prayer of a twelfth century monk as he sought to climb to the highest point within himself in order to become *there*, in the secret heart of his true self, the fulfillment of his whole complex nature. It was quite another thing to interpret and understand the Platonic psychology in the light of Aristotle's *De Anima*. For quite apart from the philosophical differences between Plato and Aristotle, the transition to Aristotelian psychology in the thirteenth century involved a further transition from the religious psychology of the early Middle Ages, dominated by a moral and spiritual interest in the study of man, to a psychology that must be properly called theoretical and speculative, dominated by the metaphysical framework and principles of Aristotle. In this transition, the

Christian Platonism of St. Augustine and of the twelfth century monks did not come to an end; on the contrary, it came to a new beginning, namely, to the time when the Platonic notions that had been used to formulate a devout and monastic Christianity were about to be reexamined in a purely philosophical way by theologians who were reading, for the first time in Christian history, the metaphysical language and teaching of Aristotle. Thus, the thirteenth century, as a new philosophical age within the Christian world —new in the sense that it was learning from Aristotle to recognize metaphysical questions in their own right and to examine them in a metaphysical way—not only revived across the centuries the doctrinal differences and conflicts between Plato and Aristotle but also codified the Platonic elements in traditional Christian thought in a way that reflected the new metaphysical understanding of the age.

Let us limit this remark to St. Thomas himself, and more specifically to the problem of the unity of man. It is possible to find in St. Thomas a comparison between the psychologies of Plato and Aristotle that does not take into account the religious use made of Platonism by St. Augustine and others and that sets forth, in the process, compelling arguments for agreeing with Aristotle as against Plato. Consider the following early text in which St. Thomas has formulated a classic and even famous comparison between the ways in which Plato and Aristotle explained the relations between soul and body:

"On the union of the soul to the body there was among the ancients a twofold opinion.

9

"According to one opinion the soul is united to the body as a complete being to a complete being, so that the soul would be in the body as a sailor in a ship. For this reason, as Gregory of Nyssa recounts, Plato held that man was not something constituted of soul and body, he was rather a soul that has put on a body . . .

"But this opinion is not tenable because, if it were, the body would be joined to the soul in an accidental way. As a consequence, the name *man*, which in its meaning embraces soul and body, would not signify something essentially one but only an accidental unity, and thus would not be a name in the genus of substance.

"The second opinion is that of Aristotle, which all the moderns follow, to the effect that the soul is united to the body as form to matter. From this it follows that the soul is a part of human nature, and not a given nature by itself." [4]

We are, then, in the age of the moderns, that is, in the world that was reading the *De Anima* and the *Metaphysics* of Aristotle. From the treatise of Nemesius *On the Nature of Man*, which he mistakenly attributed to St. Gregory of Nyssa, St. Thomas knew the Platonic definition of man as a soul using or wearing a body. Indeed, St. Thomas could have found in the obscure work of Nemesius, written toward A.D. 400, the essential elements of the fundamental debate between Plato and Aristotle on the nature of the soul and its union with the body. He could even have found a strong Platonic effort to explain the union of soul and body, and to answer, in the light of its author's dissatisfaction with Aristotle, how soul and body were united as two substances to constitute man. [5] But though he took his information on Plato from Nemesius, St. Thomas parted company with him by refusing to believe that the Aristotelian definition of the soul as the substantial form of the body made the soul material and corruptible. St. Thomas was perfectly aware of the issue at stake, and it is important to recognize that there was something un-Aristotelian in the way in which the question was asked. How can a spiritual substance be the substantial form of matter? In the *De Spiritualibus Creaturis*, St. Thomas formulated in so many words both the issue at stake and the reason for Nemesius' objection to Aristotle. Can a spiritual or an intellectual substance be joined to a body as its substantial form? Here is the crux of the difficulty:

"The difficulty in this question arises because a spiritual substance is a given reality that subsists through itself. A form, on the other hand, has the requirement of being in something else, that is, in matter, of which it is the act or the perfection. Hence it seems to be contrary to the nature of a spiritual substance that it be the form of the body. That is why Gregory of Nyssa, in his book *On the Soul*, imputed to Aristotle the view that the soul was not a reality subsisting through itself and was corrupted with the corruption of the body; the reason was that Aristotle held the soul to be an entelechy, that is, the act or perfection of a physical body." [6]

Now, however we answer the difficulty as posed, it is quite clear that the issue between Plato and Aristotle as presented by St. Thomas consists in determining whether man is the union of two whole or complete beings, namely, the soul and the body, or whether he is the union of two parts related to one another, ac-

11

cording to the principles of Aristotle, as form to matter in the constitution of a unitary substance called man. If we adopt the former alternative, it is then a question to know how we can say that the sum of two complete beings is itself a unity. And if we locate the whole essence of man in the soul in order to avoid this consequence, then we seem to save the unity of man by making the body accidentally related to him and by establishing no more than an accidental unity between man (the soul) and his body. On the other hand, if we adopt the Aristotelian alternative, we certainly guarantee the unity of man, since form and matter are related as parts in the constitution of a single substance. But what happens to the spirituality of the soul in this union? According to Nemesius —and he was far from alone in this decision—the soul could not be the form of the body without being material and therefore corruptible.

Thus, considered as a whole, the issue at stake is whether we can say at one and the same time that the human soul is a spiritual substance in its own right, having therefore its own existence, and the substantial form of the human body. The issue is a purely philosophical one at least in this sense: it seeks to know the metaphysical conditions under which the union of soul and body is to be explained in order to ensure the unity of man in his very existence as a being. But it should be perfectly clear that the issue as so formulated is domestic to the thirteenth century. Early medieval thinkers should not be made a party to an issue that they did not know, nor should their Platonism be read as a philosophical position upholding one part of what was to be a thirteenth century debate. Thus, the Platonists of the twelfth century did not intend to deny the integrity of man in magnifying the soul at the expense of the body, in speaking of the inner man and his outward garment, or in using a rich and extravagant Platonic imagery to express the way in which the soul is related to the body. The gentle William of Saint-Thierry did not mean to deny the unity of man when he said that the soul was just about the whole man: *totus quippe paene homo anima est;* for he added, in explanation, that the body was the least important part of man: *minima ejus portio corpus est.* The abbot of Saint-Thierry, after all, was not a professor of metaphysics or a theologian speaking a metaphysical language; he was a remarkable theorist of the image of God in man, and he wished to remind those who were monks of the incomparably greater dignity of the soul over the body. This is, indeed, what Abbot William said: *O imago Dei, recognoscere dignitatem tuam.*[7] It would be both difficult and forced to use the modest position of the human body within William's religious self-examination as the equivalent of a philosophical exclusion of the body from its rightful place within the economy of the human composite. Later on in the twelfth century, Godfrey of Saint-Victor, who used almost the whole range of the Platonic imagery in expressing the superiority of the soul to the body, was no less insistent on emphasizing the unity of man and of soul and body in man. If he was willing to write that the soul occupies the body as a sort of dwelling, he was also careful to say that *spiritus et caro una persona, unus homo sint.*[8]

And elsewhere he wrote: "In each man there are in a manner two things, flesh and spirit or the bodily man and the spiritual man . . . yet flesh and spirit are one and the same man." [9]

Like other thinkers of their age, William of Saint-Thierry and Godfrey of Saint-Victor did not know any Aristotelian metaphysics, they did not appreciate the Aristotelian notion of a composite substance, and they were not taking part in the thirteenth century discussion on the unity of man. So far as they knew the unity of the human person, they did not deny it. Like their contemporaries, they had great difficulty in understanding how a simple and immaterial soul was present to the body and yet not in a spatial way.[10] But this problem, which is at least as old as Plotinus and St. Augustine, not to mention Nemesius, is witness to the metaphysical innocence of the twelfth century. Between what they did not deny, if only because they did not know it, and what they asserted in their spiritual search for the true center of the human person within themselves, the monks of the twelfth century cannot be accused of violating the integrity of the human composite. Their aim was rather to magnify the soul and to suggest how, if man remembered his spiritual dignity, he could learn to hold the substance of his whole life fixed within the divine image that linked him to eternity. Indeed, the more one reads those remarkable twelfth century treatises on the soul, the more one thing becomes clear. From William of Saint-Thierry to Aelred of Rievaulx and to Godfrey of Saint-Victor, the Cistercian and Victorine monks did not know how to say with Aristotle that man was one being, or that he was one in his existence, his nature, his powers, and their order. But they knew in detail how to unify man's being in the liberating love of God and to realize that being in its fullness by teaching it to become all mind, a total memory of God. They knew, in other words, the moral and religious unification of the human person, his historical growth as a person living in time until, with the passing of time, he learned to concentrate the *I* of his turbulent reality in the single-minded love of God.

One can scarcely suppose that St. Thomas did not know or appreciate this total fulfillment of the Christian man in the divine image within him.[11] Such a fulfillment was, in fact, the historical mirror in which the philosophical theologian of the thirteenth century could see the unfolding reality of man himself, and especially the mystery of a spirit joined to matter. In this mirror the Christian man verified the compositeness of his nature, not in terms of metaphysical principles or in a metaphysical language, but in prayer and meditation. To seek and find his true self only when, at the touch of God, he finally opened his heart to the divine peace,[12] is certainly not a lesson in metaphysics; nevertheless, it is truly to discover that aspect of human nature, namely, its spiritual formlessness, which occupied, each in his own way, both the monk in his meditations and the philosophizing theologian in his interpretation of the constitution of man. From St. Augustine to the Victorines, Christian thinkers knew man as a person; they affirmed his unity as a person in the union of soul and body, but they also held the superiority of the soul over the body, and expressed it by a number of analogies that can perhaps be summarized in the language of St. Augustine, who defined man as a soul using a body or as a soul possessing a body but who was careful to add that "a soul possessing a body does not make two persons but one man: *anima habens corpus non facit duas personas sed unum hominem.*" [13] If, in a sentence popularized by Alcher of Clairvaux in the twelfth century, St. Augustine also defined the soul as "a certain substance, sharing in reason, and suited to ruling a body," [14] he certainly did not mean to deny that soul and body were parts of the human person. As he was to say in the *De Trinitate*, "Man is a rational substance composed of a soul and a body, and there is no doubt that man has a soul which is not his body, and a body which is not his soul." [15] Thus, Platonism was for St. Augustine a vehicle for expressing the superiority of the soul over the body; it was not a vehicle for excluding the body from the unity of human nature. If there was an uncertainty in St. Augustine's mind it had rather to do with the order of soul and body to one another rather than with their unity.[16] If the soul is nobler than the body and its ruler, how do you define man? This is St. Augustine's question, but it is a question directed to the economy of human nature, to soul and body as constituting a moral whole, rather than to the ontological conditions of human unity or to man as an existential whole. In this sense, the rich moral psychology of St. Augustine could serve St. Thomas as one more mirror

16

in which to see human nature unfolding in history according to its internal exigencies.

The *Confessions* of St. Augustine is not a metaphysics of human nature; it is a dialogue between its author and God. Above all, it is a dialogue in which St. Augustine examined the fabric of his own internal life, and discovered not only that he did not know himself but also, in abandoning himself in order to go out into all the byways of the world, how much his self-knowledge depended on returning to the God Who was waiting for him in the depth of his own memory—or, rather, beyond it. To know himself, St. Augustine had to find God; which is another way of saying that the Augustinian effort to know man is, even when expressed in an abstract definition, a journey to God, a journey of unification in the love of God. Such a journey expresses, in the form of a continuing dialogue with God, the human person whose nature the theologians of the thirteenth century were to be called upon to explain in metaphysical terms. And this was, as it seems to me, the exact situation of St. Thomas Aquinas. By religious profession a monk and a theologian, but a theologian who had learned how to use metaphysics within his theology, indeed to give that theology a metaphysical human frame, St. Thomas was guided in his work by two lights within him, his religious vision of the world and of man's life and his philosophical vision of that world and man himself as creatures whose whole reality moved within the existence that God had given to them. Within the religious vision of Christianity, St. Thomas saw man not only in the history of his life but also in the nature that was itself the first moment and origin of that history. In short, St. Thomas saw the metaphysical meaning of human nature in the history that embodied its religious search for spiritual unity and repose.

Such an approach to St. Thomas Aquinas supposes that the Aristotelianism of St. Thomas Aquinas was not his "philosophy," but the technical language and instrument through which he expressed his personal philosophical ideas which he then went on to use in his theology. One need not deny that St. Thomas learned philosophy from Aristotle or that Aristotle was the common teacher of the schoolmen of the thirteenth century in order to insist that the Angelic Doctor, among others, formulated highly original and sometimes even un-Aristotelian notions in the current language of the Philosopher. Why could not St. Thomas have filled the commonplace formulas of Aristotle with a new and uncommon meaning, depending on his own intuitions for their reality? Why could he not have endowed old Aristotelian notions with a strength and a depth of meaning that still baffle the historian by their seemingly innocent combination of the old and the new? In the present instance, the question is to know whether St. Thomas was not pouring new Christian wine into an old Aristotelian bottle when, following the first chapter of the second book of the *De Anima*, he joined soul and body together as form and matter, and thereby created a doctrine of the unity of man for which the modern historian can find no philosophical predecessors, Greek or Christian.

Part II

The thirteenth century, as everyone admits and repeats, is the age of the great triumph of Aristotle in the Latin Christian world. Translated into Latin since early in the twelfth century, his writings taught Christian theologians a whole new view of the world and a whole new way—a strictly natural and philosophical way—of looking at a universe that they otherwise knew very intimately in its historical concreteness. St. Augustine had been the unrivaled Christian master of the Western world, and his various writings on God and the soul, on truth and light, on creation as a spiritual language of forms speaking to man's intelligence of the God Who was their common author, had served as the substance of the religious meditation of countless monks in the West from St. Gregory the Great to St. Bonaventure. Who had not learned from Augustine to go from outward things to his inward self, there to rise above himself to the truth that was his divine teacher and master? Who had not learned to think of the world itself as speaking to man through its creaturely forms and, as by a living dialogue, leading him to the God Whose forming hand was everywhere visible in His creatures? Now, in the thirteenth century the vast and rich tradition of St. Augustine had found an eminent intellectual rival in Aristotle. I say "rival" and not "opponent," even though Augustinians and Aristotelians of various types and temperaments were to oppose one another in the course of the century. Only, if we look at the situation as St. Thomas seems to have done, Aristotle and St. Augustine did not necessarily present any cruel either-or dilemma; on the contrary, face to face with a most difficult and controversial issue, namely, the question of the unity of soul and body in man, St. Thomas created a doctrine that he was at some pains to call Aristotelian but which was a revolution as much within historical Aristotelianism as it was within the tradition of St. Augustine. Moreover, he created a doctrine that, in its spiritual framework and substance, seems to me nearer to St. Augustine than it was to Aristotle. Let us examine this point, since it will go a long way toward clarifying not only the relations of St. Thomas to Aristotle but also his own outlook as a theologian.

From Aristotle's celebrated analysis and criticism of Plato's Ideas, the reader of the *Metaphysics* could easily grasp the new and fundamental point proposed by Aristotle, namely, that in the world of Plato there could be no individual substances nor any unified essences. Platonic substances and essences were, in reality, a cluster of participations, intelligible and ordered, but constituting a hierarchical system of forms rather than a unitary substance, a sum of separate intelligible parts.[17] This criticism went very far, as it is well known, if only because it was in reality the starting point of the Aristotelian metaphysics; it grounded and made possible the notion of an individual substance having an individual essence, with a unity and integrity of being that had not been possible in the metaphysics of Plato.

It is scarcely necessary to insist on these Aristotelian doctrines or to point out the central role played by the notion of form in Aristotle's general conception of being. For him, beings are individual substances; they are not Platonic intelligibles. These individual substances are either pure forms, self-subsistent and dynamic, or forms joined to matter, in which case the unity and the nature of the resulting composite substance come to it from the form. From this point of view, just as a substance is one and whole *as* a form or *through* its form, so essence, seen as the intelligible structure of substance, is likewise one and whole and for the same reason. This decision has far-reaching consequences in the domain of composite substances. It says that the essence of a composite substance— the essence of man, to use a difficult example—is not an aggregate or sum of parts, for then it would not be something one and whole; on the contrary, rooted in the unity of the form of the substance, the essence reflects within itself the very same unity. Hence, as soul and body constitute one substance, though a peculiar one, so animality and rationality constitute one essence in man; but this they do in such a way that animality is determined to be rational, and rationality is realized as so determining it, with the result that rationality and animality are not understandable even as parts outside their mutual completion within the unity of the essence they constitute.

In using the example of man to illustrate a justly famous Aristotelian doctrine, I have meant to lead directly to the application that St. Thomas made of it. I refer to his unvarying teaching that the human soul is joined to the body as substantial form to matter, constituting a unitary being, with an essence that is as one in its integrity as the being whose essence it is is one in its substantiality. To say that soul and body in man are related to one another as form and matter is to obey, so to speak, the metaphysical law of the land for all composite substances, and specifically the law of their unity as substances. We know how strenuously St. Thomas defended the unicity of the soul as the substantial form in man, arguing "that in the individual man there is no other substantial form than the rational soul, and that through the rational soul man is not only *man* but also *animal* and *living* and *body* and *substance* and *being*." [18] One could scarcely say more. But what we do not always see in this otherwise well known teaching is St. Thomas' equally unreserved acceptance of all the metaphysical implications of the unity and integrity of essence as defended by Aristotle against the Platonic Ideas. If a composite being is one as a substance because of the oneness of its substantial form, it is one in its essence because the parts of the essence are not added to one another but are rather internally completed and determined by one another. And this implies, in the case of man, a relationship between the soul and the body that is as difficult to visualize as it has proved difficult for both Aristotelians and non-Aristotelians to formulate.

For historical reasons, this is the point that needs to be emphasized in considering the transition from Augustinianism to Aristotelianism in the thirteenth century, and especially in considering the role of St. Thomas Aquinas in the transition. To say that he accepted Aristotle's notion of the unity of substance and essence and applied this notion to man would certainly be true. To say that, in applying it, St. Thomas knew that he was opposing on metaphysical grounds the various Platonic psychologies that seemingly did not know how to maintain the unity of man's essence as seen within the perspective of Aristotelian teaching would likewise be true. But it would not be true that those who were ignorant of Aristotle's teaching on the unity and integrity of essence, and who did not think of the unity of the human composite within this framework, were denying what they did not know or, at least, did not know how to assert in this way. This point applies to the psychology of St. Augustine and his many followers who, at one and the same time, upheld the unity of the human person but did not formulate this unity with the metaphysical understanding that St. Thomas acquired from the reading of Aristotle. Those who, in the thirteenth century, with the text of Aristotle's writings before them, nevertheless chose to disagree with an Aristotelian notion, or to modify that notion in a way that upheld the spirituality of the human soul to their satisfaction, could be said to oppose Aristotle or in some sense to modify his teaching. Such outstanding thinkers as St. Bonaventure, St. Thomas Aquinas, St. Albert the Great, Siger of Brabant, not to mention any others, were all involved in the same metaphysical conversation on the unity of the human essence as seen in the light of Aristotelian principles. Such a conversation marks a new moment in the history of Christian thought, whose newness consisted both in the addition of a new doctrinal dimension to Christian teaching and in the transformation of older ideas in the light of the newly acquired Aristotelianism of the century.

St. Augustine was not a party to the philosophical discussions of the thirteenth century, he did not know the Aristotelian *Metaphysics,* and he did not formulate his own ideas with an eye on Aristotelian principles. How, then, was he to be read in an age when the theologians and the philosophers, having been exposed to Aristotelian philosophy and, in this exposure, to an awareness of philosophy itself, were raising Aristotelian questions and seeing traditional problems with a philosophical sophistication that was new and Aristotelian in inspiration? St. Thomas' answer to this question, if I have understood it correctly, involved a much greater loyalty to Augustine than his acceptance of Aristotle is ordinarily supposed to allow. Indeed, it involved something much deeper than personal loyalty, since St. Thomas seems to have been concerned not only to exclude St. Augustine from thirteenth century philosophical discussions, but also to rethink St.

Augustine in the light of these discussions and in this way to remain united to him in the fundamental spirit of his ideas at the very moment of recasting or transforming them for Aristotelian reasons.

The question before us concerns much more our understanding of St. Thomas than that of St. Augustine. Evidently, having died early in the fifth century, St. Augustine was safe from the vicissitudes of the thirteenth. Similarly, his personal teaching on God and creation, and on man and human history, was safe from the controversies of scholastic theologians. Even so, St. Augustine was the great master of the thirteenth century, rivaling and surpassing in eminence the intellectual teacher that Aristotle was to prove for the same Christian age. How could it be otherwise? The spiritual world of St. Augustine, so full of the light of the triune God, met in the thirteenth century the substantial world of Aristotle, so full of its own internal dynamism, of endless and imperishable motion and of a God (if it is permissible to speak of Aristotelian divine being in the singular) whose reason for existing was to round out the finality of nature. As St. Thomas saw it, the true problem in this meeting was not merely to reject the eternal world of Aristotle, but to profit as much as possible from the remarkable criticism that Aristotle had leveled against Plato, to bend Aristotelian philosophy to the intellectual service of Christian doctrine and, in the name of the same Christian doctrine, to use Aristotelianism in the reconstruction of the Platonic elements present in St. Augustine.

Two doctrines in particular, the one Augustinian

and the other Aristotelian, illustrate this tactical occupation in St. Thomas' mind with vivid precision. Everyone knows the Augustinian doctrine of the divine illumination and its special role in the explanation of the presence of truth in human knowledge. Similarly, everyone knows the no less famous doctrine of the agent intellect and its presumed role in the Aristotelian explanation of the origin of abstract knowledge. If the Augustinian doctrine of the divine illumination contained within itself an irrefutable truth, namely, that the divine illumination was the ultimate source of all truth, including the truth of intellectual knowledge, it also contained what to St. Thomas seemed to be a weakness, namely, its willingness to say with Plato not only that God was the source of truth but also that the world of sensible things was radically mutable, that human sensation was fallible and subject to deception, and that but for the saving presence of divine truth man would inevitably fall into error. Now, St. Thomas found in Aristotle arguments to prove against Plato that the world of sensible things was much more permanent than Augustine had believed and that the human sense was not deceived about its proper object. St. Thomas thought, therefore, that he could correct the Platonism of St. Augustine by means of Aristotle and still leave the core of Augustinian doctrine intact. Even were we to disagree with St. Thomas, the question to ask at this point is whether he could not reasonably think that he was remaining united to St. Augustine on the central issue, the divine illumination, even though it was possible and necessary in the thirteenth century to correct the Platonic metaphysics by means of Aristotle. Seen in this way, the transition from St. Augustine to St. Thomas involved an internal transformation of Christian thought whose main effect was not the correction of St. Augustine but the possibility of assimilating Aristotelianism within Christianity under the inspiration of St. Augustine. Thus, in spite of his contemporaries, St. Thomas did not think in terms of a head-on collision between St. Augustine and Aristotle. In an age occupied with the interpretation of Aristotle, but which nevertheless intended to remain faithful to the teaching of St. Augustine, St. Thomas seems to have seen no reason for refusing to improve that teaching on specific points by means of Aristotle, just as he refused to follow the easy course of involving the authority or the teaching of St. Augustine in answering technical Aristotelian questions unknown to St. Augustine himself but very much alive in the thirteenth century.

The doctrine of the agent intellect is a case in point. The Aristotelian commentators on Aristotle had debated the question raised by an elliptical sentence in the *De Anima* and had come to the conclusion that the agent intellect referred to by Aristotle was separate from the soul of the individual man, one for all men, and active as a common and external source of intellectual light. What was St. Thomas' reaction to this position of the commentators? He acknowledged that there was some truth in the proposition that there existed a single, separated, and common source of intellectual light. Interpreting the doctrine of the agent intellect in this way, moreover, you were bound to say that, seen within the framework of the Christian world, the agent intellect was none other than God Himself, creator and last end of the human intellect, its light and its beatitude.[19] But even while admitting the truth of this position, St. Thomas was anxious to point out its inappropriateness. For the question at issue was not whether God illumined every man coming into the world. Who doubted that proposition? The question was to find a working Aristotelian answer to an admittedly difficult Aristotelian question. Now, as St. Thomas saw it, the Aristotelian question was whether there was an agent intellect *within* the soul—in other words, whether the human soul was endowed with a power called the agent intellect. To make God the agent intellect was not an answer to this question; or rather, it was an inappropriate answer insofar as, by the substitution of one question for another, the sense of the original question and the issue that it involved were both distorted.

A great deal was at stake in this inappropriateness, affecting Christian thought much more than the interpretation of Aristotle. What was at stake, for St. Thomas at least, was the integrity of man as an intellectual creature. Yes or no, did man have within his nature, as a power flowing from the very essence of his soul, an intellect that abstracted universal intelligibles from the concrete things in which human knowledge took its origin? The great Avicenna had answered this question quite frankly in the negative. For him, man received his ideas, not by abstraction, but by infusion; man was the receiver, but not in any proper sense the maker or the author, of his own intellectual knowledge.[20] To St. Thomas this position was a double insult. It was an insult to man because it robbed him of the power due his intellectual nature and made of him a sort of intellectual monstrosity, namely, an intellectual being that yet could not accomplish its proper intellectual work, the formation of universal notions as the beginning of intellectual knowledge. Moreover, the position of Avicenna was also an insult to God, Who was not accustomed to being magnified at the expense of His creatures; on the contrary, the causality of His creatures, being His work as creator, showed forth the greatness of His power.[21] As a Christian theologian, St. Thomas could not but enforce these views with great energy against both Avicenna and Avicébron, and he could not but see in the present problem an issue in which to interpret Aristotle on his own philosophical grounds, and thus make the agent intellect a power of the human soul against the claims of Aristotle's commentators, was the surest way of elucidating and enforcing a truth that could not be properly or safely received into the Christian world until its Greek and Arabian interpretations had been excised on Aristotelian grounds. Was it not, then, correct and even necessary on the part of St. Thomas to exclude an Augustinian answer to an Aristotelian question if the effect of that answer was not only to obscure the Aristotelian issue at stake but also to aid and abet the occasionalism of Avicenna? And was it not likewise correct for St. Thomas to think that, by keeping Augustine out of this Aristotelian debate, he was not so much ignoring or opposing him as remaining united to him?

These questions should not be misunderstood. I am not trying to defend the Augustinianism of St. Thomas or his loyalty to the Bishop of Hippo, and still less am I trying to minimize the differences between the Platonism of Augustine and the Aristotelianism of St. Thomas. These differences are what they are, and no amount of explanatory rhetoric will change them in any way. It remains true that St. Thomas parted company with St. Augustine on many philosophical issues and that Aristotle was the main cause or occasion of that divergence. But, in the midst of these undeniable differences, let us recognize that something else is at stake in the relations between St. Thomas and St. Augustine. What is at stake is the continuity of Christian thought itself, and especially its effort to deal with Aristotelianism in the thirteenth century. As we read St. Thomas, it is often enough possible to see why he adopted this or that Aristotelian notion, since we can see both the notion itself and the evidence for it in the Aristotelian text. But it does not follow that every notion expressed by St. Thomas in Aristotelian language was itself Aristotelian; nor does it follow that St. Thomas thought so even when he did not bother to acknowledge the point. To make Aristotle a sound philosophical vehicle of Christian thought was for him much more important than the correct historical interpretation of Aristotle's text. Not that the interpretation of Aristotle was an unimportant issue; but it was an issue that took second place to St. Thomas' objective as a theologian, namely, to use Aristotle as the spokesman of what he himself wanted to say in philosophy; and this is true even when he wanted to express notions that Aristotle himself never knew, and yet to express them in the language of Aristotle.

Where, we ask ourselves, did St. Thomas find his doctrine of the unity of the human person? To say the least, it is extremely difficult to think that he found it in Aristotle, if only because the *De Anima* never deals with the question whether an intellectual substance can be the form of the body. Why is it not possible that Christianity itself gave to St. Thomas the beginning of his answer to the question? Did not Christian thinkers, from St. Augustine to the thirteenth century, know the unity of the human person? Did they not know that soul and body somehow constituted one reality, and did they not meditate on the strange life of this reality as he grew in the world of time? Is it not possible that the unity of the Christian man, seen as a historical reality living and unfolding in the world of time, was at the beginning of St. Thomas' intuition of the metaphysical unity of human nature? For there is, to say the least, a remarkable parallel between man as seen historically in the Augustinian tradition and man as visualized metaphysically by St. Thomas himself. It is that parallel to which I wish to point and whose reality I wish to emphasize; not indeed in order to strengthen the argument by mere emphasis, but in order to throw light on the doctrine itself. Let us, therefore, look at the

Thomistic notion of the unity of human nature in its main outlines, concentrating our attention on the problem of the unity of the human essence. Wherein, within the unity of its existence, is human nature one and whole in its internal integrity?

Part III

THE MOST distinctive aspect of the Thomistic doctrine of the unity of man does not need any elaborate explanation at this date, but perhaps it needs to be better understood. That man can be one being in his compositeness only if the whole composite has existence through one formal principle, namely, the human soul, is an unusual answer to an unusual question. The answer is unusual by force of circumstance; or perhaps it may be better to say that the answer is unusual because, against the Aristotelian tradition and especially the view of the great Averroës, St. Thomas thought that he could apply the Aristotelian formula of form and matter to the relations between soul and body. And certainly, if soul and body have one formal principle of existence, such that the body exists and is all that it is through the soul, then man is one being in the order of existence, and he is one substance through the soul as his substantial principle.[22] No doubt, too, since man exists, he must be possible, however strange a being he may be. But surely he is a strange being, appearing all the more so when we see him as St. Thomas has done. Not only is he like other composite substances in nature, one through the unity of his substantial principle, but this principle—the soul—also happens to be a spiritual substance in its own right. The full strangeness of man, therefore, consists in this, that, as a composite reality including an organic body within his being, he exists wholly and radically in and through a spiritual principle.

The most important fact to notice about this doctrine, over and above its anti-Averroism, is the non-Aristotelian basis upon which St. Thomas establishes his own use of an Aristotelian formula. For the Aristotelian commentators had not been able to see how any substantial form of matter could be other than material, or how any separate and subsistent form could be other than entirely separate from matter. From this it followed that a form joined to matter was corruptible and that an incorruptible form was, and could be only, separate from matter. That there could be an intellectual form that was, at one and the same time, a substance within itself and the substantial form of matter was not only a novelty within Aristotelianism but an impossible novelty as well. How, then, could St. Thomas achieve the results that he did? The answer is not far to seek, but to understand it is much more difficult than simply to locate it. The structure of Book II of the *Summa Contra Gentiles* contains the full framework of the answer as well as, in the course of its development, the answer itself. And though the development of this Book lies beyond our present purposes, it is not irrelevant to notice what St. Thomas did to the Aristotelian notion of form in order to use it as he did. In the world of Aristotle, being had been form and pure being had been pure form. But in the world of St. Thomas Aquinas, in which God was the pure act of being and creatures existed solely because He made them to be, form was the vehicle of the act of being and nothing more, and that act was as much beyond form as it was, in a unique way, the nature of God Himself. If God alone *was* by right of His nature, no creature was by right of its constitution or its form. In such a world—and it is the world of St. Thomas Aquinas—*to be* is an act beyond form, a dimension introducing the things that are to the world of being, an intrinsic dimension without which they would be nothing but with which, as through an ever-present gift, they are all that they are.[23]

The most noteworthy result of this point of view is the elimination of the entire Averroistic dilemma concerning the intellectual soul. Averroës had pondered the Aristotelian definition of the soul at the beginning of the second book of the *De Anima* and he had argued that the soul as form was the perfection of its matter. From this conclusion he had further argued that the universality of Aristotle's definition of the soul as the first entelechy of a physical organic body meant that the definition could not be applied to the intellect. The intellect (that is, the intellect that the Latinized text of Averroës called the *intellectus materialis*) was entirely unmixed, by which Averroës meant that it was not a body or a power in a body: *neque est corpus neque virtus in corpore.*[24] In other words, the intellect was absolutely unmixed with matter, and it did not belong as a form within the domain of material forms. In short, the nonmateriality of the intellect likewise involved its total separation from matter and from the conditions of matter: the intellect could not be a form that acted as an intellect through a body. Thus, the immateriality of the intellect ultimately rested for Averroës on the fact that it was a separate essence. Averroës had no principle other than the separateness of the intellect to ensure its incorruptibility; just as it seemed to him that a nonseparate form, that is, a form united to matter, could not but be a totally material form. Surely, the substantialism of Aristotle, which Averroës carried out to the letter, could lead to no other result.

The importance of St. Thomas' answer to Averroës, consequently, does not lie in any purely exegetical victory; it lies in the total transposition of the problem from the Aristotelian level of substance to the Thomistic level of being seen in terms of *esse*, the *act of being*. St. Thomas' constant argument for the incorruptibility of the soul is that, as a spiritual substance, the soul receives the act of being in itself. That act makes it to be and to be the form that it is; and since it is a subsistent form in its own right, it exists without the possibility of being corrupted.[25] This argument goes very far, since it enables St. Thomas to pass beyond the substantialism of Aristotle and Averroës. For if the intellectual soul exercises its own act of being, then St. Thomas is quite justified in thinking that the immortality of the intellectual soul is not endangered if, at one and the same time, it is a substance in

36

its own right and the substantial form of the human body. As St. Thomas pointed out to the Averroists,[26] if the soul had existence only through the composite whose substantial form it was, then as form of matter it would be no more immaterial, and no more immortal, than the body. But, as a spiritual substance in its own right, the soul transcends the very body with which it shares its own spiritual existence. Hence, the true problem is not whether the human soul can be immortal; it cannot but be immortal in virtue of its own existence as a self-subsisting form. That is why, given the Thomistic dimensions of the *actus essendi*, there can be no problem of immortality in the case of the intellectual soul. For this very reason it is likewise true, in spite of the Aristotelian tradition, that an intellectual soul—that is, an intellectual form of matter—is possible. It is possible in the sense that such a form is not contradictory within the framework of the Thomistic metaphysics, whereas it is contradictory within the perspective of the Aristotelian and Averroistic metaphysics. How can one and the same form be, at one and the same time, a nonmaterial essence and a material one? This question cannot be successfully answered on Aristotelian grounds, but it can be transcended. This is, in fact, what St. Thomas did.

The true Thomistic question therefore lies elsewhere. What kind of being is man? What kind of internal unity does he have as a composite of spirit and matter living within a spiritual existence? How can man be defined as a rational animal? What is a rational animal whose total reality is sustained within a spiritual principle exercising a spiritual existence? To

37

ask these questions can help us to locate the fundamental point in the Thomistic position on man. With the aid of Aristotle, but on the premise of transcending his metaphysics, St. Thomas Aquinas decided that man could be one being in nature if soul and body were related to one another as co-parts, that is, as incomplete members of a whole that alone could verify and explain their meaning even as parts. The human soul, therefore, though a spiritual substance in itself, yet had the incomplete nature of a part; it was by nature both a substance and a substantial form, and therefore somehow truly both a whole and a part. Of course, had the soul been merely a part, then it would have been related to the body as to a part whose presence was required for its own substantiality. But the soul was a substance in itself, and the fact that it was a part, a substantial form, was somehow the expression of the prior fact that it was a whole, a substance. To understand man, consequently, we must go beyond soul and body as parts. Admitting fully that they are parts, we must see the whole that they constitute, man, in relation to that strange whole that is also a part, the soul. How do the *soul* and *man* answer to one another as *wholes*?

It would be a disastrous simplification of the problem at stake to see in it nothing more than a desire on the part of St. Thomas to safeguard the unity of man by the device of emphasizing the notion of the soul as a part. And certainly man would not be a whole if soul and body were not truly related to one another as part to part. "No part," St. Thomas has written, "has the completion of its nature when separated from the whole. Hence, since the soul is a part of human nature, it does not have the completion of its nature except in union with the body." [27] This much of St. Thomas' doctrine is perfectly clear. Only, it is just as clear that this much of the doctrine presupposes a larger framework that alone makes it intelligible. It is the *soul as a whole* that, in explaining the meaning of the *soul as a part,* likewise explains the meaning of *man as a whole.* In other words, to see the economy of human nature we must understand wherein the whole that is man verifies in its compositeness the whole that the soul is in its substantiality.

Another way of stating this conclusion is to say that the soul as substantial form is a link between man taken as a whole and the soul in its substantiality. It is an essential link, expressive of the soul's very nature, but it is still a link. For the soul is not only substance and form but also and especially substance *as* form. It has the sort of being that both transcends matter and, in its very transcendence, needs it for the accomplishment of its work as a spiritual substance. If the soul is a substance, consequently, on the ground of its self-subsistence, its incompleteness of nature means that it is a substance "as completing the human species as the form of the body." In short, the human soul is literally substance *as* the form of the body. In St. Thomas' own precise words: *Relinquitur igitur quod anima est hoc aliquid, ut per se potens subsistere, non quasi habens in se completam speciem, sed quasi perficiens speciem humanam ut forma corporis.*[28] Within its own context, the specific aim of this doctrine is to show not only why it has to be said against Plato that the soul cannot but be the substantial form of the human body, but also how this can be so. The *how* is the key to man as seen by St. Thomas. The point that occupied him, if only because it was a new philosophical idea within the Aristotelian tradition, was to root the meaning of the soul as form in the soul as substance, and to find in the nature of the *hoc aliquid* the source and meaning of the *forma corporis*. Thus, we are invited to go from the compositeness of man to the soul as substantial form and then to the soul as substance in order to understand the unity of human nature.

Two points in particular summarize human compositeness as St. Thomas interprets it. The union of soul and body, conceived in Aristotelian terms as the union of form and matter, exists for the sake of the soul, not vice versa; moreover, to say that the soul is a substance "as completing the human species as the form of the body" is to argue that the union is a completion of the soul in its very substance: the union is not in any sense an extrinsic addition to the soul's intellectuality, as though the resulting composite is partly intellectual and partly organic in nature. Far from being an external limitation of intellectuality, human compositeness is an internal completion of the substance of the soul in the line of its very intellectuality. Hence, instead of inferring that, as composed of soul and body, man is partly intellectual and partly sensible, we are invited by St. Thomas to think that in his very compositeness man is wholly intellectual but intellectual according to the mode of that compositeness. In short, as composite, man is wholly intellectual; as intellectual, he is composite. This is the intellectuality proper to a substance that is, as intellectual substance, the form of an organic body.

In what precise sense, then, is man a composite being? If he is not a hybrid of spirit and matter, a sort of symbiotic community of spiritual and organic life, or indeed any of the famous dualisms of mind and body proposed by Descartes and his disciples,[29] what is he? The answer of St. Thomas consists in locating the fact of compositeness entirely within the intellectual substance of the soul. Human compositeness does not mean that man is *more* than intellectual in nature; compositeness is the vehicle, not of a dualism of nature, but of a particular kind of intellectuality—and, indeed, an intellectuality that is diminished by as much as man is composite. Thus, the point to be grasped in this view is the decisive role played by the notion of the soul as whole and as part: the soul as part realizes and completes the soul as whole, just as the soul as whole has the nature to be so completed. As the completion of the substance of the soul in its very intellectuality, man is himself an intellectual whole and compositeness is the mode and the vehicle of his—and the soul's—intellectuality.

A first step in seeing man from this point of view is to recognize how far we have gone in saying that the union of soul and body is for the sake of the soul. For the whole order of sensibility within man is here at stake. If the soul is joined to a body endowed with sense organs, this fact is for St. Thomas the consequence and not the cause of another fact, namely, the existence of sense powers in the soul. In other words, we cannot argue that the soul has sensible powers because it is joined to a body endowed with organs; on the contrary, we must argue that, *because* the soul has sensible powers, *therefore* it is joined to an organic body.[30] Admittedly, this decision makes the explanation of human nature more difficult, but it does no more than carry out a principle to which St. Thomas is quite clearly committed. Since, indeed, the union of soul and body is for the sake of the soul, it is even true that the body is what it is (organic, endowed with sense organs, and so on) in view of the nature and needs of the soul itself in its very substance. The present conclusion, therefore, while adding to our difficulties, also locates the source of these difficulties. Where does that source lie? It lies in an entirely mysterious fact. Though the human soul is by nature wholly an immaterial and intellectual substance, yet the intellect is only *one* of its cognitive powers: in addition to the intellect, there is the order of sensible powers. We are now in the presence of the ultimate human mystery: an intellectual nature endowed, in its very intellectuality, with both intellectual and sensible powers. Such is the human soul, by nature an intellectual substance but also needing to be, for the sake of that same nature, the substantial form of an organic body in order to exercise the sensible powers rooted within it. Thus, the human composite becomes an understandable phenomenon as soon as we see that *man* is the answer to the true mystery within him, namely, the intellectual soul, which has both intellectual and sensible powers proceeding from its nature, which is therefore in its intellectual nature both an intellectual substance and the substantial form of an organic body, and which does not have the completion of its nature as the kind of intellectual substance that it is until, in union with the body, it becomes an incarnated intelligence.

Having resisted the temptation to add soul and body to each other, let us also try to resist the further temptation to add intellect and sense to each other. If there are cognitive sensible powers within an intellectual substance, then as powers of such a substance they have a cognitive function that only its intellectual nature can explain. In this sense, they are not additions to the nature of the soul or to the power we call the intellect; they are an expression of the kind of intellectuality the soul has and, as such, the complement of the intellect. This can mean only that the human soul has the intellectual register whose proper mode of realization as intellectual is through the cooperative activity of the intellect and the sensible powers together. In their togetherness these powers form man's complete cognitive equipment, and they embody in their work the intellectual mode of operation appropriate to the human soul as at once substance-substantial form and to man himself seen as that soul in the state of the completion of its nature. If we admit with St. Thomas that the soul is substance *as* form, and consequently form *as* substance, then we are driven to recognize that all the levels and moments of human compositeness originate in the intellectual substance itself of the soul.

This is the crux of the matter. To say that human knowledge is twofold, namely, intellectual and sensible, is at one and the same time to say a truth and to commit an error—the error of bifurcating human nature in the name of its compositeness. By everything that he has said, St. Thomas believes that composition in man is a form of unity, not a kind of addition. Hence we must make some effort not to think of intellectual and sensible knowledge as constituting two cognitional orders tied together by the doctrine of abstraction. On the contrary, there are no pure sensations in man and there is no pure intellection; there is a cognition that is at once intellectual and sensible, neither just the one nor just the other nor even just the two together by juxtaposition, but the two forming a whole that can only be called an incarnated intellectual knowledge, both universal and particular, both abstract and concrete, being as intellectual not a grasp of concrete sensible singulars but an abstract and piecemeal reading of their singularity as grasped by the powers of human sensibility. If completed knowledge terminates in the actuality of what is known, then the phenomenon of abstraction is not the most typical characteristic of human knowledge, and the two-world view of knowledge that it inevitably suggests is no more than an immobilized and inert caricature of the reality itself. One need not be a Bergsonian in order to appreciate this point. On the contrary, Bergson's unceasing attack on rationalism and abstractionism may help us to see St. Thomas all the more clearly by directing our attention, not to the conceptual machinery of human knowledge nor to the moments of immobility that abstraction introduces into it, but to the intellectual life of the soul itself, to its nature and plasticity as an intelligence, and especially to that phenomenon which more than anything else reveals its intellectual signature: *spiritual mobility*, that is to say, not spiritual activity in the sense in which this notion can properly be attributed to God and to the angels, but an activity that must move and be formed in order to realize itself in the actuality of fulfilled operation.

This, as I said above, is the crux of the matter. Man is a composite of soul and body because the human soul is at once intellectual and sensible in the powers of its nature; but since this twofold power is rooted in an intellectual nature, we are called upon to reduce it to intellectual form—to a power that is in its twofoldness intellectual. What kind of intellectual power? Intellectual power *in motion*, whose external expression consists in the humble abstractive grasp of sensible things but whose internal intellectuality is, in its spiritual emptiness and poverty, the single living source of that expression.

The human soul is not composite in its nature, but that nature nevertheless explains all the forms of compositeness to be found in man. These manifestations of compositeness, moreover, far from being accommodations resulting from the union of soul and body, are no more than consequences of the nature of the soul as an intellectual substance. *Man* answers to the *soul* as whole to whole because man is the total reality prefigured in the substance of the soul. And if this means that the soul is by nature destined to be a part of man, it also means that in the unity and concreteness of his being man is no more than the soul in the fullness of its nature—an incarnated spirit, whose unity is that he is wholly spirit but spirit involved in a discursive intellectual life on the horizon of matter, in rational motion within matter, and in a progressive approach to intellectual formation and spiritual unification.

With this conclusion we rejoin both an old Christian tradition on the nature of man and a modern view made fashionable by contemporary existentialists. Man, say the existentialists, does not have a nature; he is a historical sort of being; that is, he is whatever he projects in history by his freedom, and he remains open and unfinished. And certainly time and history are somehow of the very essence of man. But how often and how persistently St. Augustine had been aware of his own spiritual chaos and formlessness, and how often he had asked God for that moment of unification that was his constant prayer! One can say of St. Augustine not only that his own life was a pilgrimage but also that his conception of man was as of a spiritual pilgrim, growing in the world of time and being gathered by God for the world of eternity. St. Thomas did not add any historical elements to the Augustinian notion of man. But he lived at a moment in history when it was necessary to give a metaphysical formulation to many cherished Augustinian doctrines and to find, in the case of man, a metaphysical formula for what St. Augustine had expressed in terms of history.

What is man? A free projection in history, much like a comet burning its way across the heavens? Assuredly he is, and he has exercised the genius of many artists who have sought to capture him, if not in his essence, at least in his passage. With St. Thomas we are aware, in a way that is unique to him, that if man is a historical sort of being, indeed the only being in the universe that is historical by nature, this trait belongs to the soul before it belongs to man. History is the signature of the soul's intellectuality, for the human soul is an intelligence living by motion at the level of the intelligibility found in matter. That is why it is a man, a temporal spirit, engaged in an incarnated intellectual life.

Part IV

LET US now turn directly to the historical problem of the origin of the Thomistic doctrine of man. The point at issue in this problem is not how much philosophical education St. Thomas received from the writings of Aristotle; the point is to recognize how far it is true that St. Thomas created the very philosophy he expressed in the language and the techniques of Aristotle. For the philosophy created by St. Thomas could not possibly exist anywhere but on Christian soil, and by its specific shape as an instrument of the *doctrina fidei* it could not live anywhere but in the mind of a theologian.

The world of St. Thomas, so enduring and dynamic in the very structure of the things that constitute it, is first and primarily a world of creatures made by God and directed by Him to a destiny beyond time. This same world contains a history in which the final end of spiritual creatures is the central issue and the mystery of the Incarnation the central event. Within the Christian framework of the world and its historical destiny, theologians for centuries before St. Thomas had described the calling of man to a supernatural beatitude, the Benedictine monks had examined the depths of his inner life in their daily meditation, and the twelfth century theorists of religious contemplation had set forth the story of his spiritual growth in the love of God. To these Christian monuments, and within their living reality, St. Thomas added a new chapter on man. In an age of metaphysical awakening, when the Aristotelian texts were raising philosophical questions to which there were no available Christian philosophical answers, St. Thomas created within his theology a theory of the unity of human nature that was religious in inspiration, philosophical in intuition, and Aristotelian in its technical analysis and exposition.

It is difficult to describe adequately a doctrine that is the fusion of such elements and that, in the last analysis, depends for its existence on the vision of its author. Between St. Thomas' theology and Aristotelian philosophy there intervened his own metaphysical insights and principles. This is certainly true in the case of man himself, whose unity and temporality as a person, so well known to Christian thinkers from St. Augustine to St. Bernard, could not be successfully expressed by the Aristotelian formula of form and matter until that formula had been taken out of the world described by the Aristotelian physics and located within the Christian world of spiritual substances. Here is the true moment of decision for St. Thomas. For the basic problem at stake was to justify the introduction of the whole order of matter and motion within the domain of spiritual substances. Certainly here was an issue whose very possibility was at odds with the foundations of historical Aristotelianism, Greek or Arabian. For Aristotle and his commentators, spiritual substances were few in number and existed solely for the purpose of keeping the world of matter and motion in endless imitation and pursuit of them. To suggest that the center of the universe was the world of spiritual substances and that the order of matter and motion existed for the sake of man and of that *longior via* which was his personal journey to maturity as well as to eternity [31] was to undo the Aristotelian perspective in physics and astronomy. But to place spiritual substances and their destiny at the center of creation required that matter, motion, and time be included within the spiritual economy of the world of which they were now a part. Merely to juxtapose the spiritual and the material within man, by simply relating soul and body to one another as form to matter, was not enough since it left the internal unity of man unexplained. Like the world of Aristotle, he still remained a two-part anomaly; he had no integrity and there was no meaning to the role of organic matter within his nature—unless that meaning were no more than the perpetuation of the anomaly itself. What was needed was nothing less than the total inclusion of the material within the spiritual in man's nature, so that what the human body contributed as an organic and material instrument was already present within the soul *in a spiritual form and as a spiritual exigency.*

51

And this was, unless I am mistaken, the point of St. Thomas' teaching on the unity of human nature. The human soul, which is a spiritual substance *as* the form of matter, is an intellectual creature destined by nature for a historical existence, for an incarnate and therefore temporal duration, in order to express and to realize the intellectuality proper to it. The human soul, in other words, is in an entirely unique way an intelligence that can *be* itself only by *enacting* within itself a personal history; it is the only intellectual creature that needs to experience a duration subject to time and motion in order to find and to build its very nature. How far this doctrine goes can be seen quite clearly if we approach it in the light of the idea that contemporary existentialists have made rather fashionable, namely, the above-mentioned paradox that man, being a person and not a thing, is the kind of reality who has a history but not a nature.

To say that man has a history but not a nature is to express the dilemma of the meaning of human nature in the most embarrassed way possible. To be sure, existentialist philosophers and playwrights wear this embarrassment very much like a badge. But, in any case, their emphasis on man as a person and on the historical character of his being has helped to bring old and profound truths into a sharper, though sometimes distorted, focus. Man is not a part of nature nor an object of science. He cannot be examined with laboratory tools, though scientists can tell us a great many things about him. He is a curious phenomenon set off against physical nature because, more than anything else, he is liberty and engagement. He remains unfinished and unknown until he reveals himself in those acts of self-commitment that express his freedom and mirror his reality. But if there cannot be an objective science of man, there can be a history. This goes very far. As an open and free person, uncommitted and therefore open, man is the sort of being whom you can put into a play, but not into a blueprint. Indeed, being free, he must somehow write a specific character within himself before he himself knows what he is; nor does he know this until he enacts it and, on stage, discovers the substance of his deepest feelings—love and despair, loneliness and the dread that goes with it, and the constant awareness and fear of death and dying. Man is thus a spirit in the state of formation, groping for self-discovery and stability, finding no response to his gaze in the world of brute nature, and aiming beyond nature toward he knows not what—perhaps heaven if you listen to Karl Jaspers, the world of Christian love if you listen to Gabriel Marcel, or the pains of hell if you listen to Jean-Paul Sartre.

We are not here concerned with the various roads to the right or to the left taken by contemporary existentialists. We are concerned with the fact that, against the positivist worship of science, they have raised the human person beyond the domain of scientific investigation. For them, in the radical and sometimes terrifying freedom of action that is his, man escapes the deterministic framework and procedures of the physical sciences. In short, there can be no objective science of man as man: there are only individual personal histories, each a world unto itself.

By an attentive reading of all that is uniquely personal, free and supraphysical in human consciousness, the existentialists have kept present-day philosophy open —and, indeed, have widened the opening—to a realm of being beyond the reach of science. In this way they have reopened the door to a living metaphysics slammed shut by Kant from the beginning of his first *Critique*.

Admittedly, this ambition to transcend nature and the world of things has succeeded in freeing man from the positivist worship of fact. This same ambition has helped to explore and measure the gulf that separates the person from the world of physical nature. It has disengaged the texture of human reality and its human relationships in all their moral character and spiritual substance, and it has revealed to philosophy a world of existence that marks a new level and a new starting point for metaphysical speculation. Here lies the great moment of accomplishment for existentialism. Here is a world of existence—existence revealed within the life of the human person—in which the use of the verb *to be* is a personal act of free projection into the future, an act of risk and commitment, suspended in a world that is never given because we always meet it as unfinished and to come within ourselves.

For St. Thomas, too, man is a strange being; moral choice is the trademark of his character on the stage of existence, deliberation and discursiveness are his intellectual signature, and history teeming and flowing with a continuous motion is the substance of his life. But for St. Thomas man's history is not at war with his nature or with nature in general, and man experiences no need to purchase his freedom at the price of saying that he does not have an essence. Indeed, his nature is not to be a defiant part of a physical universe in which he remains forever a stranger; it is to be wholly and entirely a rational spirit, incorporating the world of physical nature within his own spiritual being so that, by moving spiritually with the intelligible steps he can gather from the world of matter, he may play out a personal drama within himself. Nor does this drama consist in completing his nature by the addition of parts; it consists in gathering his formlessness, his discursiveness, and his freedom within a supreme response to the offer of beatitude that God Himself made to man when, as St. Thomas says, He crossed from eternity to the world of time in order to assure man that beatitude was possible for him.[32]

One need not press the comparison with modern existentialism in order to recognize that for St. Thomas man is by nature a historical being and that history is the very meaning of his compositeness. But the comparison has its point since it enables us to emphasize the fact that dominates his view of the unity of human nature. Instead of divorcing man from the physical world in order to emphasize that he is a person and not a thing, St. Thomas rather incorporates the world of nature within man in order to show thereby both that nature is a part of him and also that in his substance man is a spiritual pilgrim, nature is the proper instrument of his pilgrimage, and to grow by means of the intelligible rhythm found in the world of physical motion is his intellectual gait. In this sense, the slow maturing of man, his need to spend time *being* a man, is for St. Thomas no more than the outward and visible sign of a deeper and inward temporality. For thus *to be* a man is *to be becoming* one through a personal history. History is part of man's nature because he cannot be a man without becoming one, to become one is to be one in the flow and process of history, and human time is the precious substance of the becoming that is his being as a man. So understood, man is indeed the incarnate soul. He is the soul that in its substantiality is form of matter, that floods its incarnateness with the historical secret of its own intellectuality, and that gives to man as a whole his true location within the spiritual community of creation.

Thus, if it be true that Aristotle enabled St. Thomas to express both the unity and the dynamic structure of human nature, it was not Aristotle who gave him the *man* whose nature he expressed with Aristotelian tools. How could Aristotle have taught St. Thomas that history was man's incarnate intellectuality in motion if the Aristotelian astronomy had made the reality of history impossible? And how could St. Thomas have visualized using the Aristotelian doctrine of matter and form to express the unity of man as an incarnated intelligence unless he knew the temporality of nature that was the inner meaning of that unity and that intelligence? Where, then, did St. Thomas Aquinas learn the meaning of the human person?

Those who believe that Aristotle gave him the answer to this question will have to explain how the

Stagirite could have transmitted to St. Thomas a doctrine that he himself did not have or how he could have failed to transmit to him dilemmas that all his other disciples and commentators inherited from him. The *man* whose nature St. Thomas explains in Aristotle's language could not have lived in Aristotle's world. On the other hand, when he is clothed in the language of the *De Anima* the man St. Thomas describes in the *Summa Theologiae* and the *Summa Contra Gentiles* is not easily recognizable as a citizen of the world of St. Augustine. We are here at the origin of the Thomistic notion of man, and the problem is not to say too much in the teeth of the facts or too little in their absence. Whatever Aristotle was for St. Thomas, he was not the source of the doctrine of man as an incarnated intelligence; whatever St. Augustine was, he was not the source of the doctrine of man as a composite of form and matter, however much he may have defended the integrity of soul and body. There is in St. Thomas a *philosophical* doctrine of man that is neither Aristotelian nor Augustinian in nature or origin. To say too much at this point is to argue that this new philosophical doctrine owes nothing to Aristotle or to St. Augustine. To say too little is to suppose that, since we are looking for the source of a philosophical doctrine and therefore presumably a philosophical source, Aristotle must win by default because St. Augustine must lose by reason of his Platonism. What could be simpler?

But if we make an effort to say neither too much nor too little, we are left with a philosophical doctrine that owes its existence as a doctrine to St. Thomas himself, that is philosophically alien to the world of Aristotle and that expresses in its own way a reality that can be found within the world of St. Augustine even when we allow for the differences between saying that man is a composite of soul and body and saying that he is a soul using a body. What St. Augustine expressed by means of Platonic elements was not a philosophical doctrine of man but, directly and primarily, the notion of a spiritual odyssey, a history, a pilgrimage to Jerusalem. The psychology of St. Augustine was the history of a religious journey, the journey of the Christian man called to truth and beatitude; and St. Thomas remained faithful to such a man, and to St. Augustine himself, at the very moment when he substituted Aristotle for Plato in his own philosophical account of the unity of human nature. Let us emphasize this point, since the issue before us is to see, not how Plato stood between St. Thomas and St. Augustine, but wherein the two theologians were united in their view of man. *Man*, created for a beatitude beyond time, unites them in a way that is safely beyond their philosophical differences; and the continuity of their theologies is such that it is more important to notice their complementary diversities than to emphasize their philosophical differences. For whereas St. Augustine had studied man by delineating his life and his history, in the thirteenth century St. Thomas saw the necessity of giving to the religious psychology of St. Augustine not only its proper location as a concrete psychology of lived existence, but also the ontological substructure that was at the origin of that life. Man was a wayfarer by *nature* as well as by *his-*

tory, and history was no more than his nature enacting itself in time. Man's history was the story of his being and his being could be seen both revealing and fulfilling itself in history. If St. Thomas made man a genuine composite, it was not to bury the soul in the body; it was to express, with a deep loyalty and with fuller adequacy, a notion dear to St. Augustine: the incarnate soul was a peculiar spirit, a spirit that somehow needed to live in the world of matter and time in order to grow into its destiny. Whatever corrections St. Thomas introduced into Augustinianism, his purpose was to give a proper metaphysical grounding to the teaching of Augustine. To fill the Aristotelian bottle of matter and form with the life of the Augustinian wayfarer was certainly to create a new reality, the notion of man as an incarnated intelligence. This is a Thomistic creation, which, as such, has no predecessors but which expresses in the language of metaphysics what St. Augustine had expressed in the language of history. For in the Christian world, being itself, spoken by God in creation, is a kind of history; and creation itself is not only the history set forth in *Genesis*. God expressed it in the language of being before making its secret audible in human words. If He made man to live out a history on earth, He gave him a nature that was already the seed of history, needing the soil of time in which to grow. St. Augustine and St. Thomas are united at this moment, and the Thomistic doctrine of man was born in this unity.

NOTES

1. I have dealt with the general problem of this lecture in earlier discussions. See "Man as Nature and Spirit" (*Doctor Communis*, Vol. IV, 1951, pp. 52–63); "Some Permanent Contributions of Medieval Philosophy to the Notion of Man" (*Transactions of the Royal Society of Canada*, Third Series, Section II, Vol. XLVI, 1952, pp. 67–78); "St. Thomas and the Unity of Man" (*Progress in Philosophy*, ed. J. A. McWilliams [Milwaukee: The Bruce Publishing Company, 1955], pp. 153–173); "Some Reflections on *Summa Contra Gentiles* II, 56" (*An Etienne Gilson Tribute*, ed. C. J. O'Neil [Milwaukee: The Marquette University Press, 1959], pp. 169–188).

2. See A. C. Pegis, "Some Reflections on *Summa Contra Gentiles* II, 56," pp. 186–188.

3. On the religious character of twelfth century psychology, see Philippe Delhaye, *Godfroid de Saint-Victor, Microcosmus: Etude Théologique* (Gembloux: Editions J. Duculot, 1951), chapters 5–8, pp. 94–177. Note, especially, this interesting comment: "A century later, Godfrey would have taught a psychology inspired by Christian Aristotelianism. The theory of the soul as form of the body would have done more justice to his radical humanism than a Neoplatonism for which the body remains external to man, if not his enemy" (*Etude*, p. 94). For a survey of twelfth cen-

61

tury treatises on the soul, see J.-M. Dechanet, *Oeuvres choisies de Guillaume de Saint-Thierry* (Paris: Aubier, 1943), pp. 51–58; P. Delhaye, *op. cit.*, pp. 138–140; C. H. Talbot, *Aelred of Rievaulx: De Anima* (London: The Warburg Institute, University of London, 1952), pp. 32–51. From another point of view, on the pre-scholastic or pre-metaphysical aspects of twelfth century thought, see the remarkable essays of M.-D. Chenu, *La théologie au douzième siècle* (Paris: Librairie Philosophique J. Vrin, 1957).

4. St. Thomas, *In III Sent.*, d. 5, q. 3, a. 2; ed. M. F. Moos (Paris: P. Lethielleux, 1933), pp. 206–207. Cf. *In II Sent.*, d. 17, q. 2, a. 2; ed. P. Mandonnet (Paris: P. Lethielleux, 1929), pp. 431–432. The reference to Nemesius is *De Natura Hominis*, III; *Patrologia Graeca*, Vol. 40, Col. 593B. For St. Thomas' use of Nemesius as a source on the Platonic doctrine that man is a soul using or wearing a body, see also *De Spiritualibus Creaturis*, a. 2 (ed. L. Keeler [Rome: Gregorian University Press, 1936], p. 27); *De Anima*, a. 1; *De Unitate Intellectus*, I, 33; III, 76, 78 (ed. L. Keeler [Rome: Gregorian University Press, 1936], pp. 23, 47–48, 49). For Aristotle, see *De Anima*, II, 1. 412 a15–22.

The Platonic source of the notion of man as a soul using a body is *Alcibiades I*, 129e–130c. Plotinus quotes this definition as Platonic in *Enneads*, VI, 7.5 (ed. E. Bréhier, *Plotin*, Paris: Société d'Editions "Les Belles Lettres," VI, 2, 1938, p. 74), and without attribution in *Enneads*, I, 1.1 (ed. E. Bréhier, I, 1924, p. 38). The channel of the transmission of these and other Plotinian texts to pagan and Christian writers of the late fourth century and after (for example, Macrobius, St. Augustine, Claudianus Mamertus) is a controverted point. It seems more than likely, however, that lost writings of Porphyry, including Latin translations of these writings, served as an intermediate link in this transmission. See Pierre Courcelle, *Les Lettres grecques en occident* (Paris: E. de Boccard, 1943), pp. xii–xvi, 21–36, 156 ff., 225 ff.

On Macrobius' use of the Platonic formula, see *Commentaria in Somnium Scipionis*, II, 12.7–11 (in *Macrobius*, ed. F. Eyssenhardt, 2nd ed., Leipsig: B. G. Teubner, 1893), p. 625. For an English translation of this text, see W. H. Stahl, *Macrobius, Commentary on the Dream of Scipio* (New York: Columbia University Press, 1952), pp. 223–224. Stahl's translation of "animal" by "creature" is troublesome, while to render "dum a se animatur" (II, 12. 10) by "being self-moved" (Stahl, p. 224) is plainly wrong. Why not: "as long as the body is animated by it"?

For St. Augustine, see, below, Note 13.

Claudianus Mamertus (died about 474) quotes extensively from the *Phaedo* on the immortality and self-motion of the soul, and he refers to the *Alcibiades* and other Platonic dialogues; but he does not cite the definition of man as an *anima utens corpore*. See *De Statu Animae*, II, 7; ed. A. Engelbrecht (*Corpus Scriptorum Ecclesiasticorum Latinorum*, Vol. XI, Vienna, 1885), pp. 122–128.

5. Because of the historical importance of Nemesius, I have translated the relevant texts of his *De Natura Hominis* in the appendix to this lecture. See, below, pp. 73–82.

6. St. Thomas, *De Spiritualibus Creaturis*, a. 2; *ed. cit.*, p. 24.

7. William of Saint-Thierry, *Expositio Super Cantica Canticorum*, nos. 44 and 54; ed. M.-M. Davy, *Guillaume de Saint-Thierry, Commentaire sur le Cantique des Cantiques* (Paris: Librairie Philosophique J. Vrin, 1958), pp. 72, 80 ff.

8. Godfrey of Saint-Victor, *Microcosmus*, III, 154; ed. P. Delhaye (Gembloux: Editions J. Duculot, 1951), p. 172.

9. *Ibid.*, III, 163; *ed. cit.*, p. 184. Cf. III, 155, 157, 158, 159; *ed. cit.*, pp. 172, 174, 176, 177.

10. See, by way of example, Aelred of Rievaulx, *De Anima*, I; ed. C. H. Talbot, pp. 65–67. Cf. St. Augustine, *De Genesi ad Litteram*, VIII, 21.42 and 22.43; *Patrologia Latina*, Vol. 34, Col. 389. See also William of Saint-Thierry, *De Natura Corporis et Animae*, I (in J.-M. Dechanet, *op. cit.*, pp. 105–107). For Nemesius, see, below, pp. 81–82.

11. St. Thomas, *Summa Theologiae*, I, q. 93, aa. 6–8.

12. St. Augustine, *Confessiones*, 10, 27.38; *Pat. Lat.*, Vol. 32, Col. 795.

13. St. Augustine, *In Joan. Evangelium*, 19, 5.15; *Pat. Lat.*, Vol. 35, Col. 1553. On man as a soul using a body, see *De Moribus Ecclesiae*, I, 27.52; *Pat. Lat.*, Vol. 32, Col. 1332.

14. St. Augustine, *De Quantitate Animae*, 13.24; *Pat. Lat.*, Vol. 32, Col. 1048. As it is known, this definition of the soul was given wide currency in the twelfth and thirteenth centuries by the *De Spiritu et Anima*, commonly attributed to St. Augustine in the

Middle Ages, but compiled by Alcher of Clairvaux: see *De Spiritu et Anima*, I; *Pat. Lat.*, Vol. 40, Col. 781. Alcher quotes and circulates three other definitions of the soul from earlier Latin writers: see *De Spiritu et Anima*, VII, XII, XXIV; *Pat. Lat.*, Vol. 40, Coll. 784, 788, 796.

15. St. Augustine, *De Trinitate*, XV, 7.11; *Pat. Lat.*, Vol. 42, Col. 1065.

16. See especially the discussion of St. Augustine in *De Civitate Dei*, XIX, 3; *Pat. Lat.*, Vol. 41, Coll. 625–626; and the much earlier *De Moribus Ecclesiae*, I, 4.6; *Pat. Lat.*, Vol. 32, Col. 1313.

17. The classic Aristotelian account of Plato on this point is naturally *Metaphysics*, I, chapters 6 and 9 (987 a29 ff., 990 a33 ff.). See also *Metaphysics*, V, 6. 1015 b16 ff., especially 1016 a33 ff. (with which compare St. Thomas, *Summa Contra Gentiles*, II, cc. 56, 68, 69).

For recent accounts of difficulties in the Aristotelian metaphysics as both a science of being as being and a theology of separate substances, see J. Owens, *The Doctrine of Being in the Aristotelian Metaphysics* (Toronto: Pontifical Institute of Mediaeval Studies, 1951 [2nd ed., 1963]), pp. 213 ff., especially pp. 289–300; A. Mansion, "Philosophie première, philosophie seconde et métaphysique chez Aristote" (*Revue Philosophique de Louvain*, Vol. 56, 1958, pp. 165–221); P. Aubenque, *Le Problème de l'être chez Aristote* (Paris: Presses Universitaires de France, 1962), pp. 21–68.

18. St. Thomas, *De Spirit. Creat.*, a. 3; ed. L. Keeler, p. 44.

19. See the references cited at the end of this note, especially *De Anima*, a. 5.

That St. Thomas was perfectly willing to accept the doctrine of the divine illumination *on its own ground* and therefore defend the presence of divine truth in the world is quite clear: see especially *Summa Contra Gentiles*, III, c. 47, and, more generally, *Sum. Theol.*, I, q. 84, a. 6. But it is just as clear that for St. Thomas the divine illumination is present to creatures as a *creative* light, so that we are aware of its presence *both* in the constitution of its effects *and* in its own transcendent visibility within its effects. This is the point that St. Thomas makes in the text of the *Summa Contra Gentiles*. Hence, in fully admitting the visibility of God as creative cause of things, St. Thomas can think that he is in agreement with St. Augustine. Where he departs from Augustine is in the question of the internal constitution of things. God illumines man by creating him with an agent intellect, the human author of human knowledge and humanly acquired truth: see *De Spirit. Creat.*, a. 10, ad 8; ed. L. Keeler, pp. 131–133. Hence St. Thomas' insistence that, in a strict sense, it is not correct to speak of God as the agent intellect of the soul: see *De Anima*, a. 5 (the most ample text on the question); *De Unitate Intellectus*, IV, 86 (ed. L. Keeler, pp. 54–55); *De Spirit. Creat.*, a. 10 (ed. L. Keeler, pp. 126–128).

20. This is St. Thomas' standing interpretation of Avicenna: see *Summa Contra Gentiles*, II, c. 74; *Sum. Theol.*, I, q. 84, a. 4. For Avicenna, see *De Anima*, V, cc. 5–6 (*Opera* [Venice, 1508], foll. 25 rb, 26 rb); and, generally, E. Gilson, *History of Chris-*

tian Philosophy in the Middle Ages (New York: Random House, 1955), pp. 200–205.

21. St. Thomas, *Summa Contra Gentiles*, III, c. 69, §15.

22. See, in general: *Summa Contra Gentiles*, II, cc. 56, 68, 69; *Sum. Theol.*, I, q. 76, aa. 1 and 4. On the unicity of the soul: *Summa Contra Gentiles*, II, c. 58 and *Sum. Theol.*, I, q. 76, a. 3. On the impossibility of many forms in man: *Summa Contra Gentiles*, II, c. 72; *Sum. Theol.*, I, q. 76, a. 8; *De Spiritualibus Creaturis*, a. 4; *De Anima*, a. 10. On the soul as substance *as* form: *De Anima*, a. 1.

23. See *Summa Contra Gentiles*, II, cc. 46–55, and notice that throughout this discussion St. Thomas does not determine what intellectual substances are here under consideration. Indeed, all are. Then in c. 56 he begins the study of the soul, and does not reach the angels as intellectual substances until c. 91.

This procedure has two curious aspects. There is no direct study of material creatures throughout Book II. Moreover, St. Thomas devotes over four times as much space to souls as he does to angels. Anyone who argues, as A. Gauthier has recently done, that the *Summa Contra Gentiles* is a work of pure theology written for all time and without historical occupation must explain this historically burdened structure of Book II and its disproportionately long discussion of the human soul. (See A. Gauthier's Introduction to *Saint Thomas d'Aquin, Contra Gentiles*, Livre Premier [Paris: P. Lethielleux, 1961], pp. 60–123. The conclusion [pp. 121–123] is directed primarily against M.-D. Chenu's comment on the *Summa Contra*

Gentiles that "rarely was a doctrine more historical" in its location and aim [*Introduction à l'étude de saint Thomas d'Aquin*, Montreal and Paris, 1950, p. 248]. But the remark of Father Chenu still stands.)

24. On the soul as *forma* and *perfectio* in Averroës, see *Averrois Cordubensis Commentarium Magnum in Aristotelis De Anima Libros*, ed. F. S. Crawford (Cambridge, Mass.: The Mediaeval Academy of America, 1953, *Lib. II*, Comm. 5 (pp. 134^9–136^{64}, especially, p. 135^{25} ff.); Comm. 7 (pp. 138^{11}–139^{45}); Comm. 11 (pp. 147^{11}–148^{41}). These texts deal with the universality of the Aristotelian definition of the soul; they exclude the rational part of the soul from the definition, and indicate the strict unity that soul and body have; finally, they look ahead to the full resolution of the question when Aristotle will deal "de virtute rationabili" (p. 148^{32}).

The rational part of the soul is like the sense in being a passive power; but this means that it is receptive, not that, in knowing, it is subject to change. See *In Lib III*, Comm. 2 and 3 (p. 380^4 ff.; 382^6 ff.). That is why it is unmixed, being neither a body nor a power in a body: *neque corpus neque virtus in corpore* (*In Lib. III*, Comm. 4; p. 383^{8-9}). Thus there are two main propositions about the intellect: it is a passive power, but not a transmutable one (*ibid.*; p. 384^{25-30}). Thus the knowing intellect—the *intellectus materialis* —"est igitur non mixtum cum corpore omnino." For "neque est etiam aliqua forma formarum materialium; formae enim materiales non sunt separabiles" (*ibid.*; pp. 385^{78}–386^{86}). A definition of the material intel-

lect: *ibid.*, pp. 386[96-105]; Comm. 5, p. 387[7-15, 23-26].
Like matter on the score of possibility, the material
intellect is in potency to all universal material forms;
but unlike prime matter, which is as potency to all
sensible forms, the material intellect has a reception
that is distinct from the determining and limiting
mode proper to prime matter.

This distinction had two celebrated historical consequences: (*a*) One was the decision of Aristotle to
acknowledge the fact of the distinction, that is, "to
posit such a nature [the *intellectus materialis*] which
is other than the nature of matter and the nature of
form and the nature of the composite" (*ibid.*; p.
388[54-56]). (*b*) This decision led the interpreters of
Aristotle to hold that the material intellect was a
substance, neither generable nor corruptible (*ibid.*;
p. 389[57-59]). The interpreters thought likewise that
this was the view of Aristotle, and Averroës himself
agrees (*ibid.*; p. 389[63-65]). This conclusion brings to a
head a number of celebrated Aristotelian dilemmas,
and Averroës devotes the rest of the present lengthy
Commentum in trying to resolve them. Consider.

If the material intellect is one and eternal for all
men, and so is its correlative agent intellect, how is intellectual knowledge generable and not eternal? And
if the material intellect is one, why do men differ in
their acquired knowledge? Moreover, how could the
last or final human perfection of man, acquired knowledge, be multiplied according to the number of men,
if the first human perfection, the intellect, is one for
all and not multiplied? The celebrated *continuatio* is

Averroës' answer to these questions, or the principle of the answer. But let us notice the constant basis of the answer.

The material intellect cannot be multiplied; otherwise it would be a body or a bodily form or power, and its receptivity would be exactly that of prime matter. For Averroës everything hinges on this point. If the receptivity of the material intellect is not like that of prime matter, then the material intellect is entirely separated from bodies. Hence, whereas Alexander of Aphrodisias had accepted the total universality of the definition of the soul in *De Anima*, II, 1, and had consequently made the intellect bodily and corruptible, in the course of the present discussion Averroës refuses to agree with this view. For him, since the material intellect has a nonbodily receptivity, it can be called a *perfectio* only equivocally (Comm. 5; p. 405$^{527-536}$). Averroës' constant theme is: "aliae enim partes animae sunt formae in materiis, rationalis autem non" (Comm. 6; p. 417$^{99-100}$). And this is his constant corollary: "opinati sumus . . . quod intellectus materialis est unicus omnibus hominibus" (Comm. 5; p. 406$^{575-576}$).

On the relations of the possible intellect to the agent intellect in Averroës, see the summary of the state of the question in E. Gilson, *History of Christian Philosophy in the Middle Ages*, pp. 224–225, 645.

25. St. Thomas, *Summa Contra Gentiles*, II, c. 55; *Sum. Theol.*, I, q. 50, a. 5; q. 75, a. 6; *De Anima*, a. 14.

26. St. Thomas, *De Unitate Intellectus*, III, 83–

84; ed. L. Keeler, pp. 52–53. See A. C. Pegis, "St. Thomas and the Unity of Man," pp. 165–167.

27. St. Thomas, *De Spirit. Creat.*, a. 2, ad 5; ed. L. Keeler, p. 30.

28. St. Thomas, *De Anima*, a. 1.

29. For a recent discussion of the Cartesian doctrine of the relations of soul and body, particularly as compared with that of St. Thomas Aquinas, see Henri Gouhier, *La pensée métaphysique de Descartes* (Paris: Librairie Philosophique J. Vrin, 1962), pp. 321–400.

30. See St. Thomas, *De Anima*, aa. 7–8; *Sum. Theol.*, I, q. 76, a. 5.

31. St. Thomas, *Sum. Theol.*, I, q. 62, a. 5, ad 1.

32. See St. Thomas, *Summa Contra Gentiles*, IV, c. 54, especially: "Fuit igitur convenientissimum quod Deus humanam naturam assumeret ad spem hominis in beatitudinem sublevandam" (§2).

APPENDIX

Some Texts from Nemesius' Treatise

On the Nature of Man

WRITTEN AT the turn of the fifth century, twice translated into Latin (by Alfanus of Salerno in the eleventh century and Burgundio of Pisa in the twelfth), the work of Nemesius was an influential spokesman in the thirteenth century for what was to prove the standard mortalist interpretation of Aristotle's definition of the soul. If the soul is a form of matter it is itself material; the only alternative is that the soul be present to the body as substance to substance. The explanation of the manner of this presence is a remarkable effort on Nemesius' part, for which he is evidently indebted to Ammonius and Plotinus.

The text of the *De Natura Hominis* was translated into English for the first time by William Telfer (*Cyril of Jerusalem and Nemesius of Emesa* [Library of Christian Classics, Vol. IV, London: SCM Press Ltd., 1955], pp. 203–453, with running commentary). Unfortunately, the translation is often loose and difficult to use for purposes of doctrinal interpretation. The present version of three selections from the first three chapters is based on the edition of C. F.

73

Matthaei (Magdeburg, 1802), reprinted in J. P. Migne, *Patrologia Graeca*, Vol. 40, Coll. 504 ff.

I. PLOTINUS, PLATO AND ARISTOTLE

ON MAN (from *De Natura Hominis*, I;

Pat. Graeca, Vol. 40, Coll. 504A–505B).

"Many and admirable men have thought that man was most perfectly fashioned of an intelligent soul and a body, and this so artfully that he could not have been produced or constituted in any other way. But the proposition that the soul is intelligent is open to debate. Did the intellect join the soul as one being joins another and thus made it intelligent? Or did the soul, of itself and by nature, come to possess intelligence, which is, like the eye in the body, its noblest part? Some, including Plotinus, hold that the soul and the intellect are distinct from one another and that man is constituted of three things, body, soul and intellect. . . . Others did not separate the intellect from the soul; they hold that the intellect is the ruling part of the substance of the soul. Aristotle, on the other hand, believes that the potential intellect was fashioned as part of man, whereas the intellect in act comes to us from the outside, not adding to the being and reality of man, but contributing to the progress of his knowledge and contemplation of natural things. Aristotle contends that very few men indeed, and these only the men who have lived philosophically, possess the intellect in act. As for Plato, he does not seem to say that man is the pair together, soul and body, but the soul using such a body. Plato thinks that this is more befitting to what is human in man and returns us hence to the occupation and concern of the soul alone; so that, believing ourselves to be the soul, we pursue only the goods of the soul, the virtues and piety, and spurn the desires of the body as not belonging to man as man but primarily to what is animal and secondarily to man, since he is also animal."

II. AGAINST THE SOUL AS ENTELECHY

(from *De Natura Hominis*, II; *Pat. Graeca*, Vol. 40, Coll. 560B–565B).

"In calling the soul an entelechy, Aristotle nevertheless agrees with those who call it a quality. But, first of all, let us clear up what an entelechy is for him. He speaks of substance in three ways, namely, as the underlying matter, which in itself is nothing but has the potency for generation; then the shape and form in accord with which the matter is formed; finally, the composite, produced from the matter and the form, which is the resulting besouled thing. Matter, then, is potency, the form is entelechy, and this in two senses: first, as in the possession of knowledge, and second, as in the use of knowledge, that is, as disposition or as activity. The soul is as knowledge because, in its reality, it is both sleep and waking. The waking state is analogous to the use of knowledge, and sleep is analogous to the possession and non-use of knowledge. And since knowledge is prior to its use, for this reason Aristotle calls the form the first entelechy and the activity the second. For example, the eye is made up of a subject and a form. The subject is the eye itself, and that which receives the sight, or the form, is the matter of the eye. By an equivocation this matter is likewise called the eye. The form and first entelechy of the eye is sight, which gives to the eye the power to see; the second entelechy of the eye is its activity, in accord with which it sees. Just as, therefore, a newborn dog has neither entelechy [of sight], but the power to receive the entelechy, so we must understand the situation in the case of the soul. Just as the generated sight of the dog perfects his eye, so the generated soul in the body perfects the living being [the animal], so that the soul is never without the body nor is the body separated from the soul. No doubt, the soul is not a body, it is something belonging to a body; and that is why it exists in a body and a body of such a kind; but by itself it does not exist.

"Against this view it may be said first that Aristotle calls the life-giving part of the soul a soul, separating the rational part from it. But he should have taken the soul of man all together; he should not have argued about the whole from the part, and the weakest part at that. Besides, he says that the body possesses life in potency, and this prior to the coming of the soul. For he says that the body has life in potency in itself. But the body, which possesses life in potency, must first be an actual body, and it cannot be an actual body before receiving the form, since matter is formless and not a body. Therefore, it is impossible for that which is actually nothing to have potency, so that something can be generated from it. And if it be argued that the body is also a *body* potentially, how can that which is a body potentially have within itself life potentially? Besides, whereas in the case of other things it is possible to possess something but not to use it (for example, to possess sight, but not to use it), this is not possible in the case of the soul. For the sleeping man is not without the energy of his soul. He is nourished and he grows, he imagines and he breathes, which is especially a sign of life. From these arguments it is evident that life in potency cannot be present to anyone, but only life in act. For that which primarily makes the soul to be a form is nothing other than life. In the case of the soul life is something that is inborn, in the case of the body it is by participation. He who says, therefore, that health is analogous to life is not speaking of the life of the soul but of that of the body, and is thus arguing sophistically. Bodily substance is able to receive opposites in different parts of itself, but form cannot do so in any way. For if there is a change according to form, the animal itself will change. Hence, substance as meaning form cannot receive opposites; only substance as a subject, that is, bodily substance, can.

"In no way, therefore, can the soul be the entelechy of the body; it is a substance complete in itself and incorporeal. It does receive opposites alternately, for example, vice and virtue, which the form could not

77

receive. Besides, Aristotle says that the soul as entelechy is unmoved within itself but is moved accidentally. Now, it is quite possible that the soul should move us, though in itself it is unmoved. Thus beauty, though unmoved, moves us. But in that case, it remains unmoved in itself and moves us; it moves that which has the nature to be moved, and not at all that which is unmoved."

III. ON THE UNION OF SOUL AND BODY
(from *De Natura Hominis*, III; *Pat. Graeca*,
Vol. 40, Coll. 592A–601A).

"We must moreover inquire how a union of the soul and a soulless body takes place. For it is a baffling sort of thing. And if, as some hold, man is made up not only of soul and body, but of an intellect as well, the difficulty is even greater. Worse still, if man himself is something distinct from these, as others have said, then the difficulty is completely unanswerable. All things that are united in the establishment of one substance are completely united, and all things that are united are changed and do not remain what they formerly were, as will be shown in the case of the elements: united, they become something else. How, then, if the body is united to the soul, does it continue to be a body? Or how, if the soul is incorporeal and substantial in itself, is it united to the body and become a part of the living being [man], while maintaining its own substance unmixed and uncorrupted? For, of necessity, [1] either soul and body are united and are both changed and corrupted together, as are the elements; [2] or they are not united, because of the aforementioned difficulties, but are set together, as dancers in a dance or as a stone alongside a stone; [3] or they are mixed as wine and water.

"But that the soul cannot be set alongside the body has been shown in the [chapter entitled] *On the Soul.* For if it were, only that part of the body would be besouled that was near the soul; what was not joined would remain soulless. Besides, we cannot really call one the things that are merely set alongside one another, like pieces of wood or iron or the like. As for the mixture of the wine and the water, it corrupts both of them together, for the mixture is neither pure water nor pure wine; but, even so, this mixture takes place through a juxtaposition that deceives the sense by the minuteness of what is mixed. This is evident from the fact that the wine and the water can be separated from another. A sponge dipped in oil and papyrus soak up the water by itself. However, to separate physically whatever is completely united is absolutely impossible. Well, then, if soul and body are neither united nor juxtaposed nor mixed, what is the reason for which the living being is said to be one?

"This difficulty is a further reason for which Plato does not wish to hold that the living being is composed of soul and body; for him, it is a soul using a body, and as it were having put on a body. But this account, too, has its difficulties. How can the soul plus its garment be something one? A tunic and its wearer

79

are not something one. Ammonius, the teacher of Plotinus, offered the following solution to this difficulty. He said that intelligible realities have the power to be joined to those things that can receive them, for example, corruptible things, and on being joined to them remain unmixed and uncorrupted, as though separated. In the case of bodies, union brings about a complete change of those that come together, since they are transformed into different bodies—as elements to mixtures, food to blood, blood to flesh and to the other members of the body. In the case of intelligible realities, a union takes place but it is not accompanied by a change. For an intelligible reality does not have the nature to be changed in its substance; either it exists or it is corrupted to nonbeing, but it is not transformed. In point of fact, it is not even corrupted to nonbeing, or otherwise it would not be immortal. If the soul, then, being life, were transformed in a mixture, it would be changed and it would no longer be life. What, then, would it contribute to the body if it did not contribute life to it? Hence, the soul is not changed in the union.

"With this point established, that intelligible realities are unchangeable in their substance, it follows necessarily that, when they are united, they are not corrupted in the corruption of the things to which they are united. The soul is therefore joined to the body and it is joined without mixture. That the soul is joined to the body is shown by its sympathetic affection; for the whole living thing is sympathetically present to itself, as being something one. And that the soul remains unmixed is evident from the fact that in sleep, in a manner separated from the body and leaving it to lie as though dead, yet breathing just enough life into it so that it might not entirely die, the soul is active by itself in dreams, foretelling the future and living near the world of intelligible realities. The same thing likewise happens when the soul by itself contemplates some intelligible being. Then, as much as possible, it separates itself from the body and is present to itself, so that it might thus give its attention to [true] beings. For, being incorporeal, it spreads itself throughout the whole body in the manner of things that have been [thereby] corrupted, but withal remaining uncorrupted in the manner of things that are unmixed; and, preserving its own unity within itself, whatever things it touches it transforms in keeping with its own life, without being changed by them.

"As the sun by its presence transforms the air into light, making it like light, and light is joined to the air in a manner that is both unmixed and mixed, so too the soul, in being joined to the body, remains entirely unmixed. There is only this difference, that, being a body and circumscribed by a place, the sun is not everywhere its light or even its fire is found. For fire remains bound as in a place in wood and in the plantain weed. But the soul, being incorporeal and not circumscribed by a place, wholly permeates in its wholeness both its light and its body, and there is no place illumined by it where it is not present in its wholeness. For the soul is not held together by the body; on the contrary, the soul holds the body together. Nor is the soul in the body as in a vessel or a wineskin; rather, the body is in the soul. Moreover, intelligible realities are not impeded by bodies; they permeate a body in its entirety, they dwell there and they depart, and they cannot be confined by a bodily place. Being intelligible realities, they likewise dwell in intelligible places, either in themselves or in the intelligible realities beyond them. Thus, the soul is at times in itself, namely, when it is reasoning, and at times it is in the intellect, namely, when it understands. Whenever, therefore, the soul is said to be in the body, it is not said to be in the body as in a place, but as in a relationship and in a presence, as God is said to be present to us. The soul, we say, is tied to the body by a relationship, by the direction of its influence, and by its disposition; in the same way we say that the lover is bound by the beloved, not corporeally or as by a place, but relationally. Being something without dimension and bulk and parts, the soul is above the localizing containment of place. By what place can that which does not have any part be contained? For place is found with bodily bulk. It is the limit of the containing body, with reference to which it contains that which is contained. Should someone say, 'Then my soul is in Alexandria and in Rome and indeed everywhere,' he is deceiving himself in speaking once more in terms of place. For, 'in Alexandria' and, in general, 'here' are places. But the soul is not in any way in a place; it is in a relationship. For it has been shown that it cannot be circumscribed by a place.

"Hence, when the intelligible comes into a relationship with some place, or with some thing that is in a place, we say by an abuse of words that it is *there* because its *activity* is there, and we substitute place for its relationship and activity. We should say, 'The soul acts there'; we say, 'It is there.' "